T0208796

PRAYER
TIME

PRAYER TIME

*Chronicles of a Mother's Devotions
Towards the End of Life*

JACQUELYN CLAUDE AND SANDRA CLAUDE

ARCHWAY
PUBLISHING

Archway Publishing books may be ordered through booksellers or by contacting:

Archway Publishing
1663 Liberty Drive
Bloomington, IN 47403
www.archwaypublishing.com
844-669-3957

Because of the dynamic nature of the Internet, any web addresses or links contained in this book may have changed since publication and may no longer be valid. The views expressed in this work are solely those of the author and do not necessarily reflect the views of the publisher, and the publisher hereby disclaims any responsibility for them.

Any people depicted in stock imagery provided by Getty Images are models, and such images are being used for illustrative purposes only. Certain stock imagery © Getty Images.

Scripture quotations are from the Holy Bible, King James Version (Authorized Version). First published in 1611. Quoted from the KJV Classic Reference Bible, Copyright © 1983 by The Zondervan Corporation

Interior Graphics/Art Credit: Jacquelyn Claude

ISBN: 978-1-6657-3286-4 (sc)
ISBN: 978-1-6657-3287-1 (e)

Library of Congress Control Number: 2022920471

Print information available on the last page.

Archway Publishing rev. date: 11/15/2022

MY MOTHER
PRAYED FOR ME

My fondest memories of my mother are her prayers for our nation, leaders, friends, and family members. She would hold our hands before school to pray with us and instruct us to repeat the prayer with her. Each one of my siblings had a special verse from the Bible taught to us by Mom. When finishing praying over our meals, she would have each of us quote our special scripture. To this day, my verse— "The Lord is my shepherd, and I shall not want"—is incorporated throughout my life.

There were times at night I would awaken to hear my mom waging a spiritual war through prayer with our common enemy, Satan. The first time I experienced this happening, I recall asking her concerning what I heard. With those kind, gentle eyes and quaint smile, she looked me in the eye and stated, "Everything is all right, Sandy. I was attacked by Satan in my sleep and through the Holy Ghost began to wage war against the enemy in prayer." After this, she became such a spiritual giant in my young eyes.

There were times I believed Mom knew everything I was thinking or saying. But over time, I had come to realize at the age of sixteen that Mom's walk with God, that unshakeable faith, was the reason she knew so much despite only having a tenth grade education. I recall a time at eighteen years old coming home from work and handing my paycheck to my mother. I was making minimum wage, and at that time, it was $4.75 an hour. The look on my face was so hurt because I barely had any money left over. I thought she was upset with me for not wanting to hand over my paycheck. Instead, she dropped her head and replied, "Sandy, sometimes I have to cry too." I felt so low and began to see my mom also as the breadwinner, provider, father, and intercessor. She was in her fifties while having to care for three teenagers and one young adult plus dealing with life's changes of her own. She never complained and always provided an honest answer to whatever question I asked her.

Progressing through life, Mom showed such resolve and resolution when I joined the military. It was in basic training when I called home to tell Mom, "Thank you for how you raised me, because it prepared me for the trials I would face as an adult."

SANDRA CLAUDE, GRADUATION FROM
LAKELAND HIGH SCHOOL, 1993.

I went into the military without the baggage so many girls my age had experienced; I would always ask Mom to pray for my military friends. Throughout the first half of my military career, Mom's prayers helped my friends and me through some horrible situations. A ritual of mine when I called home went something like this: "Mom, did the Lord show you anything about me? And Mom, are you still praying for my friends and me?" Her reply was always yes.

Mom's prayers during those early days of my military career, for my friends and me, are forever with me. They were such a stabilizing force for us, being that many of us were on our own for the first time. Many will testify of how they did not get what they deserved because of Mom's intercessory prayer.

The last prayer I will share is of the time I was in Bosnia. I reached a low point in which I did not see myself coming home alive. I was not able to call home to tell Mom that I loved her. So I said a short prayer. "Lord, please let my mom know I love her and I died doing what I love best." I was able to call her the following day, and before I could say another word beyond "Hi, Mom," she said, "Sandy, the Lord showed me a vision of you and the amount of stress you were under, and I prayed for you." I owe my life to a mother who was sensitive enough to the working of the Holy Ghost and faithful to the call of God as an intercessory prayer warrior.

From childhood to the military, the sustaining prayers of my mother helped me to overcome the loss of my father and baby brother. She was such an inspiration to me, and I admired her greatly for her meekness and quietness when her prayers were answered from heaven on high. Unlike so many who sought to profit from their spiritual gift, Mom used her ability to intercede for others in the spiritual realm to exalt Jesus all the while testifying of his greatness. I am so thankful for the value and greatness Mom put in praying to the living God, Jesus Christ, our Lord and Savior. To this day, I can still hear my mother's prayers. I love and miss you, Mom.

A1C SANDRA CLAUDE, SCOTT AIR FORCE BASE,
UNITED STATES AIR FORCE, OCTOBER 1993.

To all mothers, I say, "Entrust your children into the hands of God, and keep them in prayer." At Mom's homegoing service, there was a floral wreath in the shape of a heart with the word "family" embroidered on a ribbon. Mom loved her family, and she loved God. Her life speaks volumes of itself. Even though it has been almost seventeen years since her passing, it feels as though she is always with me. The Lord blessed me to understand this phenomenon in December 2012. The Holy Ghost who was in her is also in me. The Holy Ghost is the promised Comforter for all born-again believers of Jesus Christ. I and so many others have become a witness.

It is an honor to share thoughts of my mom, her prayers, and little anecdotes. She was a blessing that I often had taken for granted. Thank God for His mercy and grace. This compilation of scriptures and Mom's responses to those scriptures reflect the faith and trust she exhibited in our Lord, Jesus Christ. I pray you will find encouragement in these scriptures and responses as well, to bring you over the storms of life.

Sincerely,
Sandra D. Claude

INSTRUCTIONS TO DEVELOPING A FAITH WALK

As you begin this journey with me, I encourage you to create a safe space that yields quiet time so your spirit may hear from God. Then after reading each devotion, meditate on the scriptures, write your thoughts, and set realistic goals to overcome your most difficult task. This can be achieved through daily prayer, meditation, reflection, and showing acts of charity to yourself and those around you.

To create a habit or initiate change, one must complete the task or assignment daily for at least seven days. Then begin each day fresh with reading a scripture, reciting an affirmation, and mediating on the scripture daily for strength and direction. Let's begin this journey of developing "Prayer Time" to travail through life challenges as my mother so graciously exhibited when navigating the tumultuous storms of life.

CHAPTER 1
JOY OF THE LORD

I n the stillness of the day, I heard a voice saying to me, "The joy of the Lord is your strength" (Nehemiah 8:10). As I meditated upon that scripture, my heart began to rejoice because God had heard my cry. Even in the wilderness, my faith resounds as a sounding cymbal that Jesus is my rock. I present to you an accumulation of original prayer devotions inspired by my mother, Mary F. Claude.

These writings were completed during 1998, a year before she passed on to be in the bosom of Jesus. I pray that as you read, the words will begin to speak to your wilderness and cause your faith to spring up and produce life in a dead situation.

> O death, where is thy sting? O grave, where is thy victory? (1 Corinthians 15:55)

My mother was diagnosed with uterine cancer in 1996. She had undergone a hysterectomy and radiation therapy at the time of diagnosis. However, two years later, in August 1998, the cancer advanced to endometrial cancer, stage 4. It was during this time the Lord prepared my mother for the next chapter of life, which was death from the mortal body to receive eternal rest. The devotions in this chapter are centered on joy, faith, and love in God.

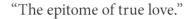

"The epitome of true love."

MARY FRANCIS (MILLER) CLAUDE JOINED IN
HOLY MATRIMONY TO FRANK DANIEL CLAUDE,
MARCH 5, 1949, PHILADELPHIA, PENNSYLVANIA.

PRAYER TIME: SCRIPTURES OF ENCOURAGEMENT WHILE IN THE WILDERNESS

What would you do if you knew your last days were near?

PRAYER TIME

And I will stretch over Jerusalem the line of Samaria and the plummet of the house of Ahab, my Lord and my God. (2 Kings 21:13)

Perfect love cast out fear. Love worketh no ill to his neighbor. (Job 4:18)

The greatest of these is charity. (1 Corinthians 13:13)

Praise the Lord, the Joy of the Lord is your strength (Nehemiah 8:10).

Thou art the apple of mine eye (Psalm 17:8, Proverbs 7:2, and Deuteronomy 32:10)

JOURNAL THOUGHTS

_____

_____

_____

_____

_____

_____

_____

_____

_____

_____

_____

_____

_____

_____

_____

_____

_____

_____

_____

_____

JOURNAL THOUGHTS

_____

_____

_____

_____

_____

_____

_____

_____

_____

_____

_____

_____

_____

_____

_____

_____

_____

_____

_____

PRAYER TIME

One would be consumed with sadness knowing in less than six months one's death in this life would be inevitable. However, that was not the case for my mother. She was faithful unto God, standing on her principles that neither life nor death would separate her from the love of God. She maintained an upbeat and positive attitude, believing unto the end that God could and would heal her. She encouraged those around her with kind words and instructed her children to love one another.

After much prayer and research, she made the conscientious decision to forego chemotherapy based on the side effects and the impact it would have on her mental capacity. My mother could remember her children and grandchildren's birthdays and recite her favorite Bible scriptures.

I remember sleeping so soundly beside my mother as she would softly awaken me with a gentle touch while saying, "Lady, it's time to get up, or you're going to be late for work." Much to Mom's chagrin, I would rather have dropped out of nursing school to take care of her. But my mother would remind me, "Jacque, I believe the Lord is calling you to be a nurse." Thus, Mom became my motivation to stay in nursing school.

Death for my mother wasn't scary. She embraced it like a soldier. She would remind me that the Lord would receive the glory out of her life either through healing her body or calling her home to eternal rest. I did not fully understand that concept at the time because I was only twenty years old. I had just started my first year of nursing school at Virginia Commonwealth University in 1998. Oh, I forgot to mention I was home on the winter break in December 1998 with my birthday fast approaching on December 30. Would I have my mother with me to celebrate my twenty-first birthday?

CHAPTER 2

STAND

P raying allows one to enter a spiritual realm where the heart speaks and the mind listens. My mother was a devout woman of God who accepted life's struggle with peace and sought God's will through prayer daily. She was a widow and mother of eighteen children, of whom sixteen survived children with one being murdered in 1993 and one child being stillborn. My father passed away from a severe asthma attack when I was ten years old. Mom was a homemaker, mother, wife, sister, daughter, niece, and saint of God. She would send notes to those she knew, testifying of the goodness of the Lord. A life steeped in prayer to the living God, Jesus Christ, molded her into a formidable Christian.

The murder of her father and deaths of a sister, husband, and children should have made my mom a bitter person. However, her faith in God never wavered but only grew stronger. Her prayer life strengthened her walk with God to face the horrific circumstances of those she loved. Though the diagnosis of cancer was difficult, she believed God would heal her body and receive the glory for her being a spiritual soldier who endured hardship faithfully. She lived by this saying: "God will give you beauty for ashes."

PRAYER TIME: SCRIPTURES OF STRENGTH AND COURAGE

"When you don't know what else to do, trust God."

But he that shall endure unto the end, the same shall be save, *praise the Lord,* not to the swift or strong. (St. Matthew 24:13)

Weeping may endure for a night, but Joy cometh in the morning, *praise the Lord.* (Psalm 30:5)

Yea, though I walk through the valley of the shadow of death, I will fear no evil. (Psalm 23:4)

Having done all to stand, *praises to the Lord*; that you may be able to withstand in the evil day and having done all to stand. (Ephesians 6:13)

The angel of the Lord encamped round about them that fear him, and delivered them, *praise the Lord.* (Psalm 37:7)

JOURNAL THOUGHTS

_____

_____

_____

_____

_____

_____

_____

_____

_____

_____

_____

_____

_____

_____

_____

_____

_____

_____

JOURNAL THOUGHTS

_____

_____

_____

_____

_____

_____

_____

_____

_____

_____

_____

_____

_____

_____

_____

_____

_____

_____

_____

_____

PRAYER TIME

How do you trust God when the path seems dark?

You close your eyes and walk by faith, hoping and praying there is an expected end. Before my mother's transition, I had a dream about my mother passing away around my birthday. In the dream, I had seen her in her favorite pink nightgown while sitting up in bed and looking so peaceful with her eyes closed. I refused to accept this dream and remained in denial despite knowing that the cancer had spread from her endometrium to her lungs. How could this happen?

Who would protect me, since both my father and brother were no longer here to serve as my protector? *God, please not my mother, my best friend who gave me hope, gave me life* was my constant thought. I was the baby of the family who would grow up without a father at the most important stages of life: teenage years. My mother had lost one set of twins at birth, and my brother—affectionately known as KC—had a twin sister named Keisha, who was stillborn. I always felt like I was a miracle baby because the Lord blessed my mother and father to conceive once again, two years after the death of Keisha, a nine-pound baby girl named Jacquelyn Dawn Claude in 1977.

The nurses would tell my mother, "You don't need to have any more children," but that didn't dismay my mother because she knew children were blessings from God. My mother experienced complications with my birth since I was a breech baby—not sure how I was turned around. My mother's last conception of life was at the age of forty-eight.

My mother lived a life of faith through the most tragic moments of time. She was born Mary Francis Miller on June 20, 1933, in Orangeburg, South Carolina, to Alice Evans

(Shuler) and Morgan Miller (my grandfather who I never had the opportunity to meet). I do not know much about my grandfather, who was brutally murdered in Trenton, New Jersey. However, from a letter I found—written by him in 1971 to my mother—I could tell he loved his "Mary Dear" and his grandchildren.

LETTER FROM MY GRANDFATHER,
MORGAN MILLER, WRITTEN IN 1971

GOOD TIMES. MOM'S FAVORITE HOLIDAY WAS
CHRISTMAS. MOM IS SITTING ON THE LEFT, DIANA
WHITE IS STANDING IN MIDDLE, AND SITTING
ON THE RIGHT IS CONSTANCE (A.K.A. CONNIE)
BAGLEY. TWO OF MY OLDER SISTERS ARE ENJOYING
FELLOWSHIP AT THE HOUSE OF MY BROTHER
DOUGLAS AND HIS WIFE, BRENDA CLAUDE,
IN SUFFOLK, VIRGINIA, DECEMBER 1995.

CHAPTER 3

GOD IS MY REFUGE

By the blood of Jesus Christ, His love is upon my soul,
Taking control of my thoughts,
And now my life is made whole.
My change is in my praise.
My change is in my worship.
Now life seems easier since Jesus transformed me
With love, peace, and joy.
I can patiently wait on my Savior.
The victory has been won.
My change is in my praise.
My change is in my worship.
Your grace has made the way straight.
Trouble is all around me,
But God's mercy prevails.
It's good to know You love me so,
And I love You.
Traveling down this journey,
I must face obstacles along the way.
But I hear Jesus saying,
"Hold on, be strong, and don't fret, My child.
I love you."

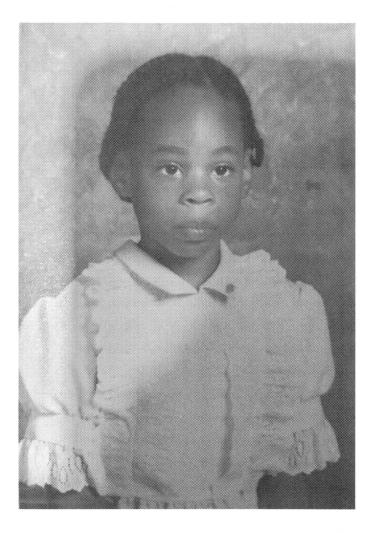

FIRST DAY OF KINDERGARTEN. My first
day of school, 1983, Elephant's Fork
Elementary School, Suffolk, Virginia.

I SURVIVED HIGH SCHOOL. I GRADUATED FROM
NANSEMOND RIVER HIGH SCHOOL, SUFFOLK,
VIRGINIA, JUNE 1996. I MADE IT THUS FAR
BECAUSE MY MOTHER PRAYED FOR ME.

PRAYER TIME: SCRIPTURES OF HOPE, FAITH, AND HEALING

"Live by faith and believe God can do any and everything."

PRAYER TIME

Praises to the Lord

Praises to God from whom all blessings flow, for it is the Lord thy God that healeth thee.

> For I am the Lord that healeth thee, praises to God. (Exodus 15:26)

> Let us forgive those who trespass against us, praise the Lord. (Luke 17:4)

PRAYER TIME

Cast all your care upon Him. The eternal God is your refuge. Underneath His everlasting arms, you have the victory forever.

> They that wait upon the Lord shall renew their strength. (Isaiah 40:31)

> God shall wipe away all tears from your eyes, praise the Lord. (Revelation 7:17)

> Cast all your cares upon him. (1 Peter 5:7)

Weeping may endure for a night, but Joy cometh in the morning, but Joy cometh in the morning, praise the Lord. Lift Jesus up, draw all men unto me; praises to Jesus of Nazareth. (Psalm 30:5)

The Holy Ghost quickened within me. Weeping may endure for a night, but joy comes in the morning.

JOURNAL THOUGHTS

JOURNAL THOUGHTS

PRAISES TO
THE LORD

I could hear my mother saying, "Now I am complete. I may move and operate because love is the guiding factor of spiritual gifts. No more a sounding brass but a song filled with melody." How does one rejoice when death is imminent? You rejoice knowing that to be absent from the body is to be present with the Lord. My hope is built on nothing less than Jesus Christ and His righteousness.

In Hebrew numerology, the number 4 is associated with the word *door*. The Lord was guiding my mother into another door of rest. She imparted words of wisdom into all her children and grandchildren. Thus, on January 1, 1999, her last words were "I am going to be OK," and then there was silence with the last peaceful breath of life. The peace of life was passed onto me as I helplessly cried out to God, "Mommy is gone, and what am I going to do now?"

I did not realize how throughout my life my mother was preparing me for life and salvation with God. I was the last born and the last one to be with my mother. The legacy of Mary F. Claude continues today. May she ever be remembered as a woman of faith. As a result of my mother's devotion to Jesus, the Word of God, prayer, and maintaining a walk of faith, I gave my life to the Lord Jesus Christ, according to Acts 2:38, on May 10, 1999.

PRAYER TIME: SCRIPTURES OF REDEMPTION AND SALVATION

When you find Jesus, you find holiness.

PRAYER TIME

For his anger endures but a moment, in his favor is life. (Psalm 30:5)

Finally, my brethren be strong in the Lord and in the power of his might. (Ephesians 6:10)

House founded upon a rock, *praise the Lord.* (St. Matthew 7:25)

Butter and honey shall he eat, that he may know to refuse the evil and choose the good. (Isaiah 7:15)

Put thou my tears into thy bottle. (Psalm 56:8)

Seek ye first the kingdom of God and his righteousness; and all these things shall be added unto you. (St. Matthew 6:33)

Trying of your faith, *praise the Lord.* (James 1:3)

Bless the Lord, O my soul and forget not all his benefits, *praises to the Lord.* (Psalm 103)

Let the redeemed of the Lord say so. (Psalm 107:2)

JOURNAL THOUGHTS

_____

_____

_____

_____

_____

_____

_____

_____

_____

_____

_____

_____

_____

_____

_____

_____

_____

_____

JOURNAL THOUGHTS

CHAPTER 5

PREPARATION

A
s the last child of eighteen, my mother would always say to me, "You will understand when you get saved." I used to ignore it because at that time I was not ready to live a devoted life unto God. I feared God but was not committed to God. My mother's life, trials, and disappointments taught me how to trust God, endure hardships, be patient, and love the most difficult people. Even though my mother was initially diagnosed with uterine cancer, she encouraged me to pursue my nursing degree at Virginia Commonwealth University in Richmond, Virginia, in 1996. I didn't realize how sick my mother was until August 1998 when she was diagnosed again, after remission, with Stage 4 endometrial cancer with six months to live.

My mother had me research the use of chemotherapy, and with prayer and fasting, she decided to forego chemotherapy. Her trust was in God to heal as the ultimate answer either by a spiritual healing or a natural death. Despite the outcome, my mother was not afraid of death because she knew God would get the glory and heaven would be her eternal home.

Two months before my mom passed, the Lord showed me in a dream her actual passing away, which would occur around my birthday. She was sitting up in bed with a peaceful look in a pink and white nightgown, just as the Lord had showed me in my dream.

I did not want to accept the truth, but it came to pass on January 1, 1999, two days after my birthday. I was in the bed with her, which is the most vivid memory I have of her death. I thought I was going to lose my mind, but God's grace kept me. Now I appreciate the dream because it gave me closure with peace of mind to know she is at eternal rest.

It's through the woman life is given and revealed. It's through the man life is created. A perfect union of two individuals to produce a seed unto God. Desire beauty that reflects spiritual maturity and personal dignity.

"Happy birthday, Jacque. You graduated from Virginia Commonwealth University, School of Nursing, on May 25, 2002, with a Bachelor of Science degree in nursing." The best part was having my grandmother Alice Evans by my side in honor of her daughter and my mom.

I MADE IT TO BSN, RN, VCU
SCHOOL OF NURSING, 2002.

PICTURED ON THE LEFT IS ME, CLASS OF 2002,
SEATED IS MY GRANDMOTHER ALICE EVANS, AND
STANDING IS MY BROTHER DOUGLAS CLAUDE.

CHAPTER 6

THE WORST ADVICE WE'VE EVER HEARD ABOUT FAITH

G oing through life, someone has given their advice on what faith is or how to obtain faith. But sometimes that advice can be misleading. For example, there is a cliché that says, "Name it and claim it." One would assume that just saying you will receive a new house, a new car, etc. means it will magically appear. Well, not exactly true. From the teachings of my mom, I learned this: "Now faith is the substance of things hoped for and the evidence of things not seen" (Hebrews 11:1 KJV). To further explore faith is to believe one may achieve a task, but it's necessary to boldly overcome obstacles to achieve it and put forth effort to receive it. You do not initially know the outcome, but trust and believe in God to make a way.

As believers, fear is the major factor that hinders one from knowing the fullness of God. For example, one might not travel for fear of flying and therefore miss out on great opportunities of visiting amazing places. On a spiritual note, one may fear what other people perceive and therefore will not operate fully in the gift from God. Trusting God moves out fear, which leads to a place of contentment.

Faith is seen as something abstract, never associated with application. Often you will hear, "You gotta have faith," without showing what faith looks like or how to apply faith. First, we must define faith, and then we must view the application of faith. For example, faith without works is dead, which is clearly an application of one's faith that can be seen as a bridge over troubled waters. What you are hoping for puts your faith on display. By grace we are saved through faith.

Faith is the building block of our initial walk with God. One must believe God is a rewarder of those who diligently seek him. In order to understand completely, one needs the power of the Holy Ghost to unlock the Word so it can become life. When you have faith, you begin to move and act according to the measure of faith. Whatever we do, the guiding factor must be love because God is love. We must love God the same way He loves us by loving our neighbors and even our enemies as being a witness to this dark world. Faith shouldn't stand in the wisdom of people but in the power of God.

The Lord is not slack concerning His promise as some count slackness but is longsuffering to us-ward not willing that any should perish but that all should come to repentance (2 Peter 3:9).

PRAYER TIME

Your faith will expedite your blessings.
(Hebrews 11:6)

What advice have you received about faith?

How do you apply faith to your life?

JOURNAL THOUGHTS

_____

_____

_____

_____

_____

_____

_____

_____

_____

_____

_____

_____

_____

_____

_____

_____

_____

_____

JOURNAL THOUGHTS

Jesus knows our needs and where to meet us. Be honest. God knows our hearts.

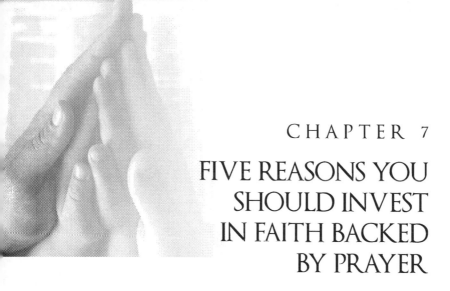

CHAPTER 7

FIVE REASONS YOU SHOULD INVEST IN FAITH BACKED BY PRAYER

1. The ROI (return on investment) is beyond measure.

Watching my mom exercise her faith through prayer helped to shape my belief in God. I developed a deeper love for prayer once I was able to comprehend the concept of believing in what you pray for. Though I prayed earnestly for God to heal Mom, I also believed that this may not be God's will. Throughout the whole process, God comforted me concerning Mom's cancer. Witnessing the entire ordeal and being her caregiver is the foundation of my nursing profession. I always have that experience to draw on when facing inevitable situations. Thus, God did answer my prayer in a way that only He knew would benefit me in the long run.

Sandra Claude

2. To have faith is free.

It is one thing to pray for healing and another thing to accept the fact that God has heard my prayer. Maybe it would be easier if faith did cost. Then I could rely on my natural ability to trust God for my prayer. However, this is not the makeup of our Christian faith. The door to faith is open and solidified through prayer. I remember my mom's prayers as a teenager. Throughout the turbulent years, my mother's faith in her prayers to God never wavered for a second. Each prayer answered increases one's faith, and prayers delayed or not answered add a framework around faith. Faith is not magical, nor is it a candy apple. It is a law that governs every believer's life. Mom exemplified faith through her prayer life by serving as an example of faith in action through prayer.

Looking back over the years since Mom's passing, I find myself reflecting more of Mom in my own prayer life.

Sandra Claude (daughter)

3. In the darkest moments, faith becomes light.

Faith is love, the God kind of love. I watched my mom in pain and agony. She couldn't find a peaceful resting place. I began to pray and placed my hand on my mom's leg as instructed by God to pray for my mother. This touch released my mom's pain. I had faith to trust in God for a miracle. I couldn't watch my mother suffer and at that moment cried out to God, "Lord, You have to do something." My faith became light by producing a miracle of God relieving my mother's pain.

Jeffery Claude (son)

4. Faith builds a solid foundation.

In faith, there is a sacrifice that one may never understand: God is using the sacrifice to get our attention. I realize now my mom's death was a sacrifice to help her children develop a personal walk with God.

5. Faith Leads to Experience, Hope and Growth (Hebrews 3:14).

For we are made partakers of Christ; if we hold the beginning of our confidence steadfast unto the end. The Divine Creator, our Heavenly Father, summons, consecrates and empowers the chosen believers. One must have a personal encounter, a spiritual resurrection that's birth in our soul. Thereby transforming one's life to be a living testament of overcoming the life of sorrows and producing a polished, priceless pearl for God's Glory. Our beloved mother, matriarch and courageous role model in Jesus, Mary Frances Miller Claude. Well done our Queen of Faithfulness!

Diana White (daughter)

Prayer reflection: How are you investing in faith?

JOURNAL THOUGHTS

_____

_____

_____

_____

_____

_____

_____

_____

_____

_____

_____

_____

_____

_____

_____

_____

_____

_____

JOURNAL THOUGHTS

Are you investing in faith?

How are you increasing your faith?

Printed in the United States
by Baker & Taylor Publisher Services